UNDERSTANDING ARTIFICIAL INTELLIGENCE: CLASS I

DR DHEERAJ MEHROTRA

Contents

Preface

Dear Young Learners,

Welcome to the fascinating world of Artificial Intelligence (AI)! This book is designed especially for you, our curious Class I students, to help you understand what AI is and how it touches our lives magically daily. Have you ever wondered how your favourite voice assistant answers your questions or how your tablet shows you cartoons you might like? That's all because of AI! Through this book, we'll take you on an exciting journey to discover the amazing things AI can do and how it helps make our lives easier, smarter, and more fun.

In this book, you will Meet AI and learn how it thinks and works. Explore real-life examples of AI, like robots, innovative toys, and apps. Enjoy fun activities and colourful illustrations that make learning about AI simple and exciting. Learning about AI will spark your imagination and inspire you to think creatively about the future.

So, let's dive into this wonderful world of Artificial Intelligence and have fun learning together. Happy Learning!

Author

CHAPTER ONE

WHAT IS ARTIFICIAL INTELLIGENCE?

What is Artificial Intelligence?

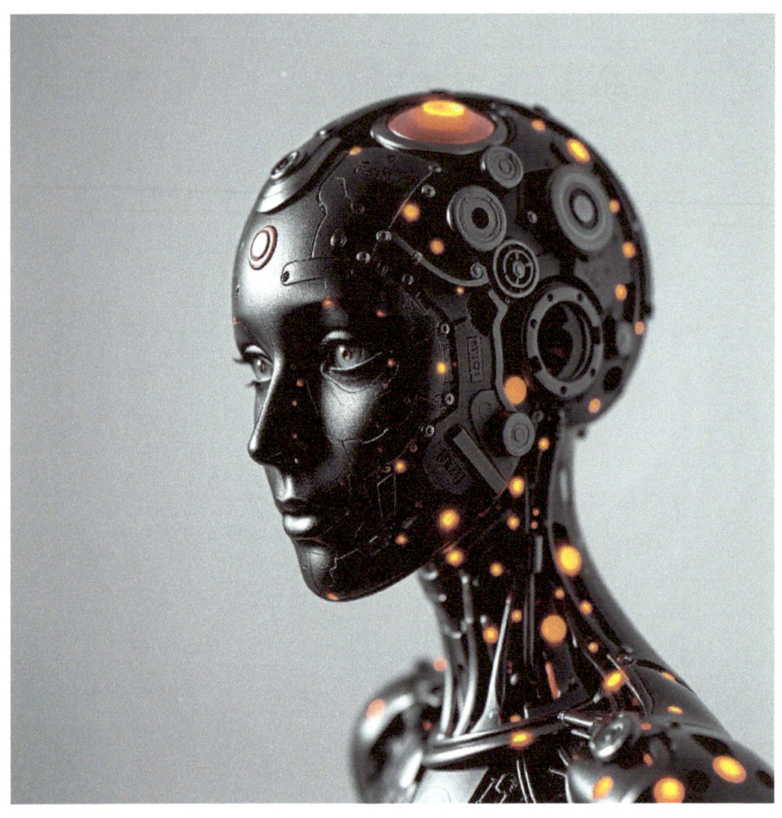

Artificial Intelligence is a branch of computer science that focuses on creating machines that can perform tasks that usually require human intelligence. These tasks include understanding language, recognizing pictures, solving problems, and making decisions.

Imagine you have a robot friend. If this robot can understand your words, play games, or even help you with homework, it uses AI!

AI allows computers and robots to learn from experience like we do.

How Does AI Work?

AI works by using a lot of data and unique algorithms. Data information that helps to learn.

For example, if we want to teach an AI to recognize animals, we would show pictures of different animals. The AI would then look at these pictures and learn to identify what makes a cat a cat or a dog.

Algorithms are like recipes that tell the AI how to process this data. They help the AI figure out patterns and make decisions based on what it has learned. The more data the AI has, the better it can become at its tasks!

Why is AI Important?

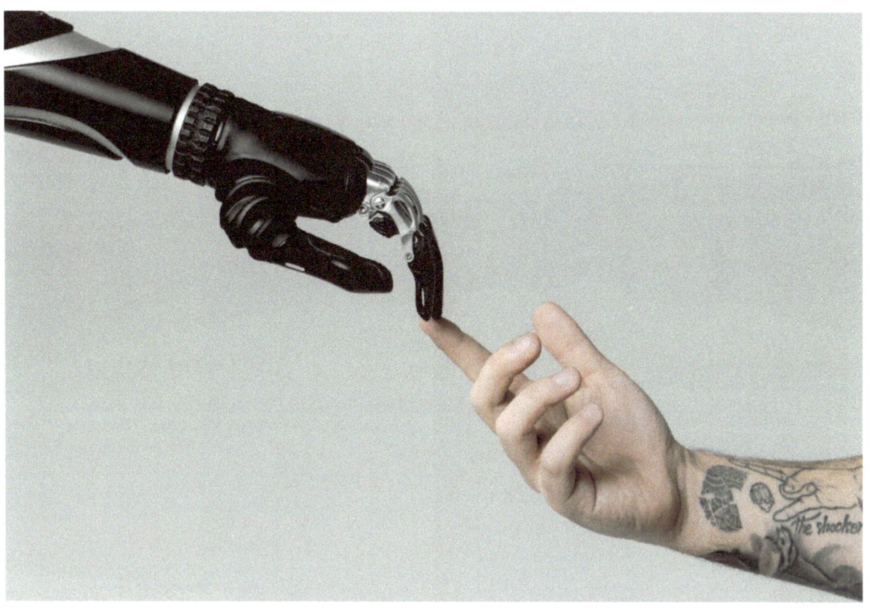

Artificial intelligence, or "AI," is the ability for a computer to think and learn. With AI, computers can perform tasks that are typically done by people, including processing language, problem-solving, and learning.

AI is important because it helps us in many ways. Here are a few examples:

Making Life Easier*: AI can help us with daily tasks, like setting reminders, playing music, or even controlling smart home devices.*

Improving Healthcare*: Doctors use AI to help diagnose diseases and suggest treatments, making healthcare more effective.*

Enhancing Learning*: AI can create personalized learning experiences for students, helping them learn at their own pace.*

Entertainment*: AI is used in video games and movies to create realistic characters and environments.*

Artificial Intelligence (AI) is a powerful tool changing how we live and work. Understanding the basics of AI allows us to appreciate how it impacts our lives and the future of technology. In the next chapter, we will explore different types of AI and how they are used in various fields.

Questions & Answers

1. What is Artificial Intelligence?
Answer: Artificial Intelligence is a branch of computer science that focuses on creating machines that can perform tasks requiring human intelligence, such as understanding language, recognizing pictures, solving problems, and making decisions.

2. What are some tasks AI can perform?
Answer: AI can understand language, recognize pictures, solve problems, and make decisions.

3. How does AI learn to recognize animals?
Answer: AI learns to recognize animals by showing pictures of different animals and identifying patterns defining each animal.

4. What are algorithms in AI?
Answer: Algorithms are like recipes that tell the AI how to process data, figure out patterns, and make decisions.

5. Why is data necessary for AI?
Answer: Data provides information that helps AI learn and improve its task performance.

6. Name two ways AI makes life easier.
Answer: AI makes life easier by setting reminders and controlling smart home devices.

7. How is AI used in healthcare?
Answer: AI is used in healthcare to help diagnose diseases and suggest treatments, improving the effectiveness of medical care.

8. What role does AI play in education?
Answer: AI creates personalized learning experiences, allowing students to learn at their own pace.

9. How is AI used in entertainment?
Answer: AI is used in video games and movies to create realistic characters and environments.

10. Why is it important to understand the basics of AI?
Answer: Understanding the basics of AI helps us appreciate its impact on our lives and the future of technology.

CHAPTER TWO

HOW DOES AI LEARN?

"AI is like a robot friend who learns to help you better every day!"

How Does AI Learn?

AI learns by looking at lots of examples, just like we do!

For example:

- *If you show a computer many pictures of cats, it learns how to recognize cats.*

- *If you play games with a computer, it can learn how to play better and even beat you sometimes!*

This process is called **machine learning***.*

The more it practices, the brighter it becomes.

AI learns by examining many examples, like when learning new things. Imagine you are learning to recognize different animals. If someone shows you many pictures of cats, you will start to understand what a cat looks like.

You notice that cats have pointy ears and whiskers and often say "meow." Similarly, when we teach a computer about cats by showing it many pictures, it learns to recognize cats, too!

Fun Example of Playing Games with AI:

Another fun example is playing games. When you play a game, you learn the rules and how to play better each time. If you play a game with a computer, it can also learn from you. The more it plays, the better it gets! Sometimes, it might beat you because it has learned all the best moves.

This whole process of learning from examples is called **machine learning**. *Just like you get better at things the more you practice, AI becomes smarter the more it learns.*

So, the next time you see a computer recognizing a cat or playing a game, remember that it has been learning just like you!

Questions & Answers

1. How does AI learn to recognize cats?
Answer: AI learns to recognize cats by being shown many pictures of cats and identifying patterns like pointy ears and whiskers.

2. What is the process of AI learning from examples called?
Answer: The process is called machine learning.

3. How does AI get better at playing games?
Answer: AI gets better at playing games by playing repeatedly, learning the rules, and improving its moves.

4. What does AI need to learn new things?
Answer: AI needs many examples, such as pictures or experiences, to learn new things.

5. What happens when a computer plays games with you repeatedly?
Answer: The computer learns from each game and becomes better, sometimes even beating you.

6. How is AI's learning similar to how humans learn?
Answer: AI learns by looking at many examples and practising, just like humans do when learning something new.

7. What features of cats does AI learn to recognize?
Answer: AI learns to recognize cats by recognizing features like pointy ears, whiskers, and the sound "meow."

8. Why does AI improve the more it is practised?
Answer: AI improves by identifying patterns and learning from repeated experiences, similar to human practice.

9. What is an example of AI learning from games?
Answer: AI learns the rules and strategies of a game by playing it repeatedly, and it becomes better over time.

10. What can you compare AI's learning process to?
Answer: AI's learning process can be compared to how humans practice and improve their skills by learning from examples.

CHAPTER THREE

WHERE CAN WE FIND AI?

Artificial Intelligence (AI) is everywhere and plays a significant role in our daily lives. From the devices we use to the games we play, AI helps make things easier and more fun. Here are some places where AI helps us:

- **Voice Assistants**: Like Siri or Alexa, they answer questions and play music.
- **Games**: AI helps make video games fun and challenging.
- **Smart Cars**: AI can drive cars by itself!
- **Schools**: AI can help teachers by grading papers and helping kids learn better.

Voice Assistants

Have you ever talked to Siri or Alexa?

These voice assistants are like friendly robots that can answer your questions, play your favourite songs, and even tell you jokes! They listen to what you say and help you find information quickly. It's like having a helpful friend right in your home!

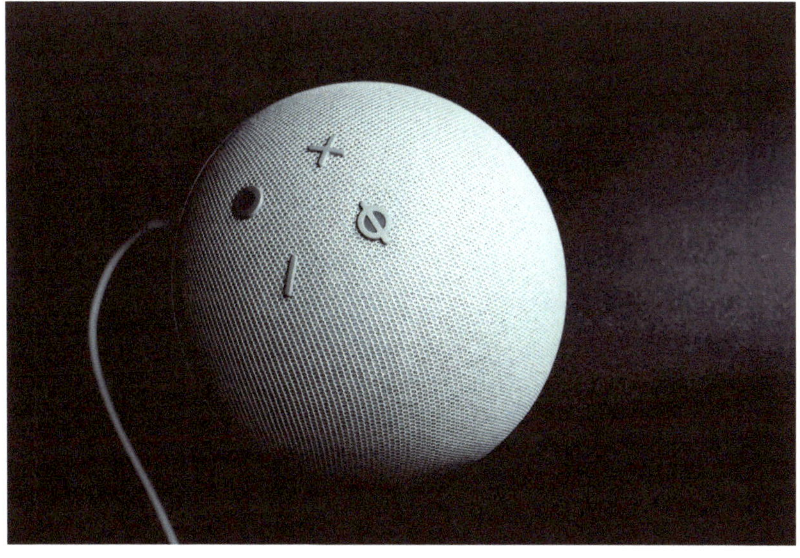

"The secret to AI's success is teamwork: humans teach it, and it helps us!"

Games

When you play video games, you might notice that some characters are brilliant and can challenge you. That's because of AI!

It helps create fun and exciting games by making the characters act cleverly. So, every time you win a game, remember that AI is working hard behind the scenes to make it enjoyable!

Playing with AI in games is like competing with a clever friend who never stops learning.

Smart Cars

Imagine a car that can drive itself! Sounds like magic, right? Well, it's AI that makes this possible. Smart cars use AI to understand their surroundings, follow traffic rules, and safely take you to your destination.

One day, you might ride in a vehicle that doesn't need a driver!

"AI shows us that even machines can learn, just like kids!"

Schools

AI is also helping in schools! Teachers can use AI to grade papers faster and give students personalized help. This means that kids can learn in a way that suits them best. AI can even help with fun learning games that make studying more exciting!

India's first AI teacher robot, Iris, was developed by Makerlabs Edutech in collaboration with the National Institution for Transforming India (NITI Aayog).

"Think of AI as a magic helper that never stops learning."

In conclusion, AI is everywhere, making our lives easier and more fun. Whether through voice assistants, video games, smart cars, or in schools, AI is here to help us learn and play!

Questions & Answers

1. What are voice assistants like Siri or Alexa used for?
Answer: Voice assistants like Siri or Alexa answer questions, play music, and tell jokes.

2. How does AI make video games more enjoyable?
Answer: AI creates intelligent characters to challenge players, making the games fun and exciting.

3. What makes a car drive by itself?
Answer: AI allows smart cars to understand their surroundings, follow traffic rules, and drive without a driver.

4. How does AI help teachers in schools?
Answer: AI helps teachers by grading papers faster and giving personalized assistance to students.

5. What is India's first AI teacher robot called?
Answer: India's first AI teacher robot is called Iris.

6. How do smart cars use AI?
Answer: Smart cars use AI to analyze their surroundings, follow traffic rules, and ensure a safe ride.

7. How does AI make learning more exciting in schools?
Answer: AI helps by providing personalized help to students and offering fun learning games.

8. Who developed the AI teacher robot Iris in India?
Answer: Iris was developed by Makerlabs Edutech in collaboration with NITI Aayog.

9. What role does AI play in voice assistants?
Answer: AI enables voice assistants to understand spoken words, answer questions, and perform tasks.

10. Why is AI considered everywhere in our lives?
Answer: AI is used in devices like voice assistants, games, smart cars, and schools, making our lives easier and more enjoyable.

CHAPTER FOUR

FUN ACTIVITIES WITH AI

Fun Activities with AI

- **Drawing AI**: *There are apps where AI can draw pictures with you.*

- **Talking AI**: *Chat with a robot or voice assistant and ask it funny questions.*

- **Games**: *Play games where AI is a player and see if you can win.*

Whether you're interested in drawing, chatting, or gaming, there's something for everyone to enjoy with AI!

Drawing AI

"Learning with AI is like having a smart teacher and playful friend in one."

One of the most creative ways to interact with AI is through drawing applications. There are various apps available that allow you to collaborate with AI to create unique artwork. You can start by sketching a simple outline, and the AI will enhance it with colours and patterns or even complete the drawing for you.

This activity encourages creativity and helps you see how AI can interpret and expand on your ideas.

Talking AI

Have you ever wanted to have a conversation with a robot?

Talking AI, such as voice assistants or chatbots, can provide a fun and interactive experience. You can ask them funny questions, tell jokes, or even engage in silly conversations.

This activity entertains and helps you understand how AI processes language and responds to different prompts. It's a great way to practice communication skills while laughing well!

Games

Playing games with AI can be both challenging and entertaining. AI acts as a player in numerous games, and you can compete against it. Whether it's a strategy game, a trivia quiz, or a puzzle, trying to outsmart the AI can be a thrilling experience.

This activity teaches you about AI decision-making and problem-solving while providing hours of fun. You can always strive to improve your skills and see if you can beat the AI!

In conclusion, engaging with AI through drawing, talking, and gaming offers a variety of fun activities that can enhance your learning experience. So, dive into the world of AI and discover its endless possibilities!

Questions & Answers

1. What can you do with Drawing AI?
Answer: You can collaborate with AI to create unique artwork, such as sketching an outline and letting AI enhance it with colours and patterns.

2. How does Talking AI provide a fun experience?
Answer: Talking AI, like voice assistants or chatbots, can engage in funny conversations, answer questions, and tell jokes.

3. What can you learn from playing games with AI?
Answer: Playing games with AI teaches about AI decision-making and problem-solving while being entertaining.

4. What type of activity is Talking AI best suited for?
Answer: Talking AI is great for practising communication skills and having interactive, fun conversations.

5. How can Drawing AI enhance creativity?
Answer: Drawing AI can interpret your sketches, add colours and patterns, or complete drawings, sparking creativity.

6. Can AI be a player in games? If yes, how?
Answer: Yes, AI can play strategy games, trivia, or puzzles and provide a challenging opponent.

7. What skills can you improve by playing games with AI?
Answer: You can improve your problem-solving, strategic thinking, and decision-making skills.

8. Why is Talking AI a fun way to understand language processing?
Answer: Talking AI shows how AI interprets language and responds, making learning about language processing enjoyable.

9. What is a unique feature of Drawing AI apps?
Answer: They can transform a simple outline into a detailed, colourful artwork.

10. How does interacting with AI through games benefit users?
Answer: It provides a fun challenge and helps users learn how AI makes decisions and solves problems.

CHAPTER FIVE

WHY IS AI IMPORTANT?

Why is AI Important?

"The secret to AI's success is teamwork: humans teach it, and it helps us!"

AI helps us in so many ways! It:

It makes work faster and easier.

It helps doctors take care of sick people.

It makes learning more fun and exciting.

AI is like a magic tool that makes the world a better place. But we must use it wisely and for good things. Artificial Intelligence, or AI, is crucial in our lives today! It helps us in many wonderful ways. This document will explore how AI makes our work faster and easier, helps doctors care for sick people, and makes learning more fun and exciting. AI can improve the world like a magic tool, but we must remember to use it wisely and for good things.

AI Makes Work Faster and Easier

"AI is like a robot friend who learns to help you better every day!"

Imagine you have a big puzzle to solve. It can take a long time to put all the pieces together. But with AI, we can solve puzzles much faster! AI can help us do our homework, organize our tasks, and even help us find information quickly. This means we can spend more time playing and having fun!

AI Helps Doctors Take Care of Sick People

When someone is not feeling well, doctors must discover what is wrong. AI can help doctors by quickly analyzing a large amount of information. It can help them make better decisions about how to help their patients feel better. This means more people can get the care they need and get better faster!

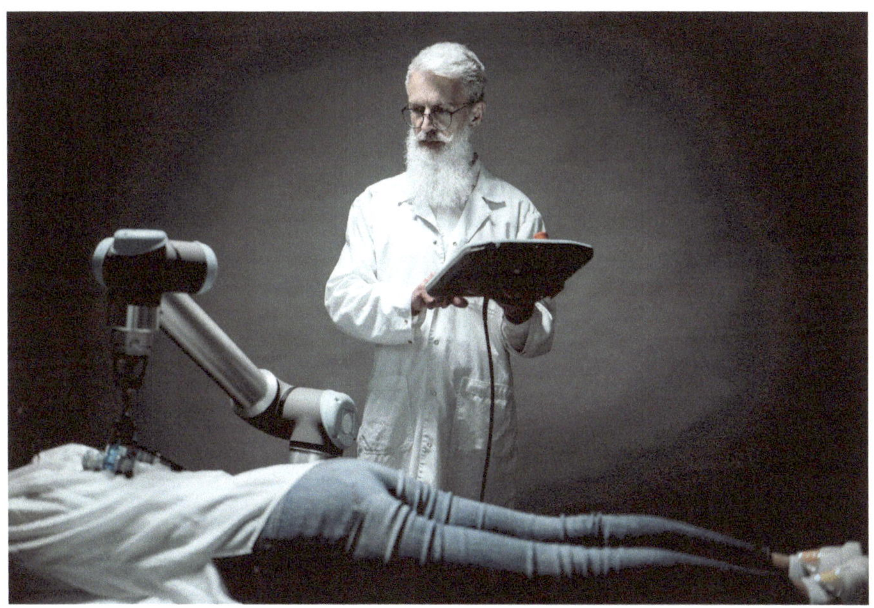

AI Makes Learning More Fun and Exciting

Learning is an adventure, and AI can make it even more exciting! With AI, we can play educational games, watch fun videos, and explore new topics interestingly and engagingly. It helps us learn new things and discover the world around us in a fun way!

Using AI Wisely

While AI is like a magic tool that helps us, we must remember to use it wisely. Like any tool, it can be used for good or bad. It is essential to use AI to help others and improve the world.

In conclusion, AI is vital because it helps us work faster, assists doctors in caring for patients, and makes learning fun. Let's use this magic tool wisely and for good things!

Glossary:

- **AI (Artificial Intelligence):** A computer's innovative problem-solving method.
- **Machine Learning:** How computers learn by practising and looking at examples.
- **Voice Assistant:** A competent helper like Siri or Alexa who talks to you.

Activity :

Draw your robot and give it a name. What will your robot do to help you?
List three ways you think AI can make school more fun.
Ask a voice assistant a question and write down the answer it gives.

Questions & Answers

1. How does AI make work faster and easier?
Answer: AI helps by solving problems quickly, organizing tasks, doing homework, and finding information faster.

2. How does AI assist doctors in taking care of sick people?
Answer: AI analyzes large amounts of information quickly, helping doctors make better decisions and provide care faster.

3. How does AI make learning more fun and exciting?
Answer: AI enables educational games, fun videos, and engaging ways to explore and learn about new topics.

4. What is one example of how AI helps in education?
Answer: AI provides educational games that make learning fun and interactive.

5. Why is it important to use AI wisely?
Answer: Like any tool, AI can be used for good or bad, so it's essential to help others and improve the world.

6. What should we remember when using AI?
Answer: We should use AI wisely for good things that benefit everyone.

7. What is a Voice Assistant?
Answer: A voice assistant, like Siri or Alexa, is a helpful AI tool that talks to you and assists with tasks like answering questions or playing music.

8. What is Machine Learning?
Answer: Machine learning is how computers learn by practising and looking at examples.

9. Can AI help doctors analyze information? How?
Answer: AI can quickly analyze much medical information, helping doctors diagnose and treat patients more effectively.

10. Why is AI compared to a magic tool?
Answer: AI is often compared to a magic tool because it can help solve problems, assist doctors, and make learning fun in extraordinary ways.

Books By The Same Author

www.authordheerajmehrotra.com